Beautiful Isles
CAYMAN

by Paul Humann

HE HATH FOUNDED IT UPON THE SEAS

Hobbies and Books Ltd., Grand Cayman, Cayman Islands, B.W.I.

PREFACE AND ACKNOWLEDGMENTS

Upon moving to the Cayman Islands in 1972, I found the people to be warm, friendly and helpful. It has been a continuing pleasure to live and work with them. This book, a compilation of pictures I have taken over the years, is a testimonial to the Caymanian people and their beautiful islands.

I wish to thank my many friends and acquaintances for their assistance in making this book possible. Naturally, several individuals and groups come to mind because of their special efforts and contributions toward this project. They include: the former Governor, Peter Lloyd and Mrs. Lloyd for their advice and counsel in several matters; Adrien and Bonnie Briggs for allowing Sunset House to become my unofficial residence on numerous occasions; Cayman Airways for providing air transportation; Steve Foster of Cico/Avis for providing an automobile on several occasions; Marjorie Bodden of Executive Air Services for assistance in getting aerial photographs; Gay Jackson, Clerk and all the Members of the Legislative Assembly; Ena Blanch Allen, Clerk of the Courts and Appeals Court Justices Edward Zacca, James Kerr and Kenneth Henry; Mike Emmanuel and the Southern Cross Club; Capt. Connie Edwards; Sheldon Hislop, Director of Civil Aviation; Florentino Gonzalez and Michael Adam of Cayman Airways; Pete and Katie Moore; John Bostock; Marcia Bodden; Joyce Hilton; Gailya Coe; Randy Davidson and Treasure Island Resort; and the staff of the Cayman Turtle Farm. Finally, I wish to especially thank the many individuals who allowed me to photograph them so the world would know what wonderful people reside in the Cayman Islands.

PHOTO ACKNOWLEDGMENTS

I wish to thank and acknowledge the Government Information Service for use of the picture of H.M. Queen Elizabeth on page 67; Wayne Hasson for use of his photograph of a Cayman Airways 727 over George Town on page 32, and the *Cayman Aggressor* on page 43; Rick Freshee for use of his photograph of the submarine on page 40; and Miguel Escalante for his photographs of the Governor on pages 67 and 68.

Paul Humann

CREDITS

Publishers/William H. & Mary A. Adam and Paul Humann
Editor/Mary A. Adam
Art & Deisgn/Paul Humann
First Printing 1986
Second Edition 1988
ISBN #0-936655-02-X, hard cover
ISBN #0-936655-03-8, soft cover
Printing by Arcata Graphics/Kingsport

Colour Separations by Florida Color Graphics, Jacksonville, Florida
Copyrighted © 1986 by Paul Humann
All rights reserved.
No part of this book may be reproduced without prior written consent.
Published by Underwater Specialists Ltd. for:
Hobbies & Books Ltd.
P.O. Box 900
Grand Cayman, Cayman Islands, B.W.I.
Ph. 1-809-94-92818
Cover: *World Famous Seven Mile Beach*

CONTENTS

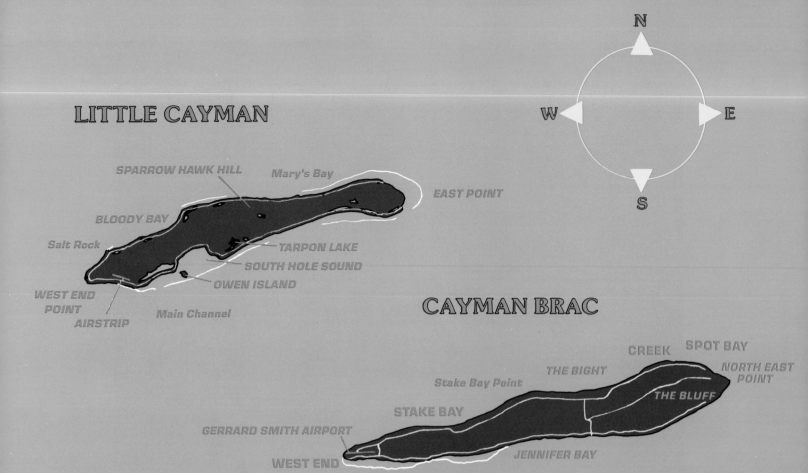

LITTLE CAYMAN

N
W — E
S

SPARROW HAWK HILL — Mary's Bay

EAST POINT

BLOODY BAY

Salt Rock

TARPON LAKE

SOUTH HOLE SOUND

OWEN ISLAND

WEST END POINT

AIRSTRIP

Main Channel

CAYMAN BRAC

CREEK — SPOT BAY

THE BIGHT

NORTH EAST POINT

Stake Bay Point

THE BLUFF

STAKE BAY

GERRARD SMITH AIRPORT

WEST END

JENNIFER BAY

SOUTHEAST BAY

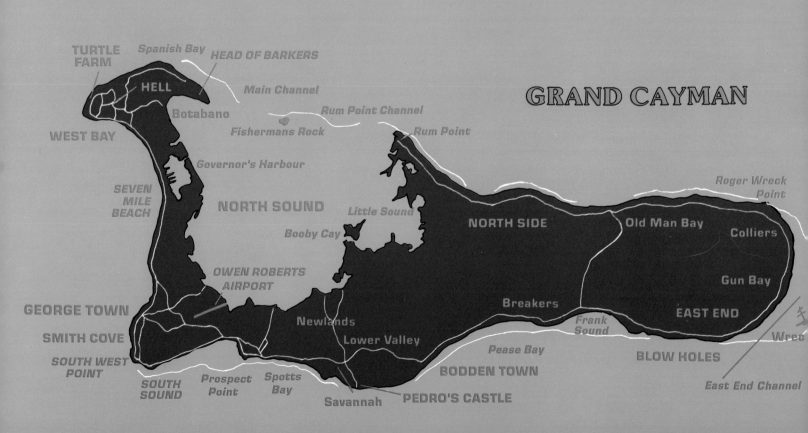

GRAND CAYMAN

TURTLE FARM

Spanish Bay

HEAD OF BARKERS

Main Channel

HELL

Botabano

Rum Point Channel

WEST BAY

Fishermans Rock

Rum Point

Governor's Harbour

SEVEN MILE BEACH

NORTH SOUND

Little Sound

NORTH SIDE

Old Man Bay

Roger Wreck Point

Colliers

Booby Cay

OWEN ROBERTS AIRPORT

Gun Bay

GEORGE TOWN

Newlands

Breakers

Frank Sound

EAST END

SMITH COVE

Lower Valley

Wrec

SOUTH WEST POINT

Pease Bay

BLOW HOLES

SOUTH SOUND

Prospect Point

Spotts Bay

BODDEN TOWN

Savannah

PEDRO'S CASTLE

East End Channel

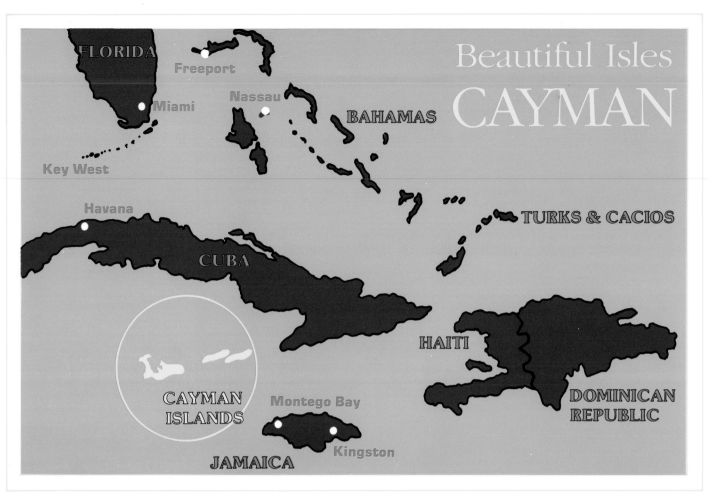

Beautiful Isles
CAYMAN

FLORIDA
Freeport
Miami
Nassau
BAHAMAS
Key West
Havana
TURKS & CACIOS
CUBA
HAITI
CAYMAN ISLANDS
Montego Bay
DOMINICAN REPUBLIC
Kingston
JAMAICA

The flag of the Cayman Islands — proudly displayed.

On May 10, 1503, during his fourth and final voyage to the New World, Christopher Columbus spotted two tiny specks on the horizon. Without setting foot on land, he claimed them for Spain. His son, Ferdinand, noted in the ship's log, "We were in sight of two very small and low islands full of tortoises, as was the sea about, insomuch that they looked like little rocks, for which reason these islands were called Tortugas." Upon learning that other islands had already beed designated "Tortugas", the name was changed briefly to "Los Lagartos", Spanish for lizard. This name apparently came from the native iguanas found in abundance on the islands at that time. Today, they are almost extinct — the majority being found in remote areas on Little Cayman. By 1527, however, the name became the Cayman Islands, the reason for which has been lost in the mists of time. Some speculate that the name is derived from "caiman" meaning alligator in Spanish. There is evidence that, although not present today, crocodiles did once inhabit these islands. Others theorize that the name came from the word "cay" which was used especially in the West Indies to describe a small coral island. In any event, the two islands Columbus spotted became Little Cayman and Cayman Brac (meaning bluff). Both are long and narrow, approximately ten miles by two miles. Lying some 60 miles to the west is the third and largest of the trio, Grand Cayman. It is approximately 22 miles long by eight miles at its widest point on the west end of the island.

Unlike most islands in the West Indies, there was no native Indian population and no evidence of inhabitation prior to their discovery. Like the origin of the name, the identities of the first residents are shrouded in the archives of history. It is probable that they were European deserters from Oliver Cromwell's army which was kept in Jamaica under deplorable conditions in the mid 1600s. Whatever their origin, life was made difficult not only by the natural elements and lack of fresh water, but by raiding pirates as well. The Cayman Islands were a notorious landfall for pirates, including Blackbeard and Henry Morgan. Here they rested, worked their ships, loaded up on turtles as a fresh meat supply and, like all good pirates, buried loot for safekeeping. Rumours and fables of treasure still abound on the Islands today. Slaves first joined the settlers in 1734, taken from the shipwreck of the *Nelly*. They were exchanged to islanders for salvage work done on the wreck. Slavery never really took hold on the Islands and was never the inhumane problem that it was in other countries. In fact, a child of a white master and black slave was called "free coloured," and, in time, was free and could even own slaves himself. Slavery was completely abolished in 1833 by British mandate.

The population of the Islands remained small throughout what are termed the "years of isolation". The islanders survived on what they could make and grow themselves. What few outside goods there were came from trade with passing ships or from the wrecks of ships that floundered on Cayman reefs. In fact, the Cayman people were once reputed to be "wreckers" because of their attempts to lure unsuspecting passing ships onto the reefs so they could salvage them for their goods. A favourite method was to put a light on a donkey and walk it down the beach, making it appear as another vessel to passing ships. Hopefully, taken in by the ploy, a ship would turn and head for the conjured illusion and crash into the intervening reef.

Not until well into the 20th century was there any regular trade, commerce or communication with the outside world. Although the first post office came to Grand Cayman in 1889 and to Cayman Brac in 1898, it could take months for mail to travel in or out of the Islands. Only occasionally did ships visit. It wasn't until 1934 that a regular means of communication arrived via the wireless service. Phones started appearing in 1937, but overseas phone calls by radio were difficult, at best. In 1966 Cable and Wireless established a local and international tele-communications service for the three islands. Finally, scheduled transportation to and from the Islands began in 1952 when PBY airboats began air service on a somewhat irregular basis. Then, in 1954, the airport on Grand Cayman was finished and ushered in a whole new era.

The original homes built in the Cayman Islands were sturdy structures supported with timbers of native mahogany and ironwood. The floors were usually hard woods, but occasionally they were of crushed rock filled with lime plaster. The walls were made of wicker work called "wattle" which was covered by lime plaster called "daub". Roofs were framed with strong rafters and covered with palm leaf thatching. The house typically had a large central living area with private sleeping quarters at either end. The window spaces had no glass, but were covered with a solid wood shutter in inclement or cool weather. Several fine examples of the "wattle and daub" houses, well over 100 years old, can still be seen, although the thatch roofing has long since disappeared in favour of corrugated steel sheets. Houses in the 75-year-old range added front porches and were often trimmed with hand-wrought lace-like fretwork. Two-story versions had a central outdoor stairway leading to a balcony onto which the sleeping quarters opened. Most of the old public and governmental buildings have disappeared, but the old courthouse still remains on the waterfront as a good example of early construction.

For years, historians have speculated over the source of the name Cayman. One of the more prevalent theories was that it was a derivative of the Spanish word "caiman" meaning alligator. Because the existence of live alligators was unknown, it was surmised that the name was a mistaken identification of the once abundant native iguana population. Today, the iguanas are almost extinct; the majority of the remaining few are found in the bush on Little Cayman.

Recent discoveries of crocodile bones such as those found in a natural well by Blair Smith have led historians to now believe that the name did indeed come from the word "caiman", having reference to a previously unrecorded crocodile population.

In years past, the people of several districts in the Cayman Islands developed unique methods of marking their graves. In Little Cayman, for example, graves were marked by a low wooden enclosure and a carved wooden head plaque.

At Spotts and in George Town, they built lime plaster monuments that resembled above-ground burial vaults that were inset with carved wooden head boards. These graves are often erroneously identified as pirate graves.

A tradition that persists even today in West Bay and surrounding areas is the outlining and decorating of graves with conch shells.

Traditional style homes in Cayman, many well over 100 years old, had window openings without glass but solid wooden shutters instead. The doors were split so the upper half could be left open to allow ventilation. The roofs were originally thatch palm, but have been replaced today with corrugated steel sheets. Most were built with lime plaster, but some were wood. Later, homes were trimmed with handwrought lace-like fretwork, and porches were added. These homes are often brightly painted and landscaped with beautiful flowering plants. Especially in the West Bay area, there is a tradition of using raked white sand, rather than grass, in yards.

In the early part of the 20th century, when two-story homes started appearing, the stairway was centered on the outside front of the house and led to sleeping quarters on the upper floor (right).

A colourful home in East End (below) displays handwrought fretwork. William Ryan, curator of the Cayman Brac Museum, displays a wooden mortar and pestle dated 1887 (below right).

One of the few homes that survived the 1932 hurricane in Cayman Brac (opposite top). The oldest remaining Government building in the Islands' capital, George Town, is the old Courts Building. Its red roof still predominates the waterfront landing area (opposite bottom).

SCENIC CAYMAN

The Cayman Islands are three emerald green jewels set in an aquamarine blue sea. They are basically low, flat and composed of porous limestone. Rain water is absorbed by the limestone or held in brackish swamps and a few ponds. There are no rivers or streams to carry mud or debris to the sea and cause it to be murky. Thus, the sea remains clear and is the greatest scenic attraction in the Cayman Islands. Whether viewed from the tranquil lee of the west, or looking out toward the prevailing swells of the southeast, or even at the storm waves of the north, the sight is absolutely breathtaking. Out at sea, the blues pass through a full range of hues, ranging from the virtually colourless, clear water at shore to the brilliant electric blues of water over sand, and ending with the deep cobalt blue of the depths.

The shorelines around all three islands have beautiful sand beaches ranging in size from secluded little coves to the world famous Seven Mile Beach on the west coast of Grand Cayman. Between the sand beaches are stretches of what is called "ironshore". Ironshore looks much like dark volcanic rock, but is actually limestone that has been eroded into sharp aberrant shapes by wave action and rain water. Frequently, small undercut chambers are formed in the ironshore by wave action. Occasionally, these chambers are connected to the surface by air passages. As waves roll in, air trapped in these chambers is compressed and pushed out the passageway with great force, blowing water high into the air like a geyser. These spectacular displays are called "blow-holes". Several good examples of this phenomenon can be viewed along the road to East End in Grand Cayman. In a few areas, the shoreline is formed by limestone bluffs. On Little Cayman and Grand Cayman, these bluffs are relatively low, rarely exceeding 25 feet in height. On Cayman Brac, however, the entire eastern third of the island is formed by a magnificent bluff rising an impressive 120 feet straight up from the sea.

The interiors of the Islands include a variety of landscapes. Mangrove swamps, starting at or near the shoreline, especially around North Sound on Grand Cayman, are refuges for a wide variety of flora and fauna, including a number of water birds. Higher interior land is overgrown by dense tropical foliage. Here, one may find exotic bromeliads, several species of endemic orchids and numerous other wildflowers. A number of rare birds are also found, including the colourful native Cayman Parrot. Higher elevations near the centers of the Islands may have low brush and stands of picturesque palm trees, including stately royal palms.

The limestone base of the Islands has created several other unique scenic wonders. In some spots, rain water has eroded the stone into lava-like configurations, much like the ironshore. In the district of West Bay, on Grand Cayman, eroded spires of limestone stand five feet high and resemble the flames of a huge fire. Appropriately, the area is named Hell. You can view these phenomenal rock outcroppings from an observation platform behind the Hell Post Office. In a few places, underground limestone caves have been formed. The best known are in the bluffs of Cayman Brac. Some of these caves are quite large and include spectacular formations. It is rumoured that these caves contain pirate booty; consequently, most have been carefully explored from one end to the other by those with a thirst for gold.

Man-made scenic attractions on the Islands include many new modern homes and buildings. Not wishing the Islands to become another Miami Beach, planners have wisely restricted building heights to no more than five stories. Older buildings are often lushly landscaped with royal palms, flowering trees and bushes. It is obvious that Caymanians nurture the beautiful plants that are found around their homes with tender loving care.

One cannot ignore downtown George Town with its unique blend of building designs. Many structures display period charm, although only a handful are original. These structures are mixed in with a variety of buildings, ranging from typical bank and office structures to the ultra-modern homes of the Legislative Assembly and Courts. The waterfront includes the commercial dock, cruise ship passenger landing area and docking areas for deep sea fishing boats and other pleasure craft. The remainder of the waterfront is primarily ironshore, with one delightful little golden sand beach where local youths still come to play and swim.

The West Indian Club (opposite) was the first condominium on the world famous Seven Mile Beach (next two pages).

Blow Holes

Strange rock outcroppings at HELL

Mangrove roots are reflected in the still waters of a swamp.

Swamp areas are a haven for many species of water birds.

Beach at tranquil South Sound

Native Cayman Brac orchids   *Schomburgkia thomsoniana* var. minor

Lisianthus   *Eustoma*

Shamrock   Butterfly Pea
Tecoma stans   *Clitoria ternatea*

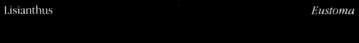

Shower of Gold   *Cassia siamea*

Spider Lilies   *Hymenocallis latifolia*

Bay Vine *Ipomoea pes - caprae, sap brasiliensis*

Frangipani *Plumeria ruba* and *pudica*

Corato Plant   *Agave sobolifera*

Cayman Brac

Fisherman in cat boat below the Cayman Brac Bluff

There are many small, beautiful caves on Grand Cayman and Cayman Brac.

Cayman Lizard

Silver Thatch Palm

Royal Palms in the wild

Native Cayman Parrot

Ocean view from the Queen's Highway on the north side of Grand Cayman.

Drying fishing nets, East End

Cat boat in mangroves at South Sound

One-of-a-kind home built of conch shells. North Sound Road, George Town

There are many new, modern homes in the Cayman Islands.

Unique home at Gun Bay.

LIME TREE BAY is one of several recently developed areas to offer a protected waterfront.

Replica of old Bodden Town guard house.

SMITH COVE is a favourite place for both tourists and Caymanians to relax.

ELIZABETHAN SQUARE, one of the many shopping and office areas in Grand Cayman.

Hog Sty Bay in George Town is a very busy place on the days of cruise ship arrivals.

Cayman Airways 727 coming in over George Town.

A spectacular Cayman sunset.

Long before the Cayman Islands were well known as a general tourist destination, banking haven or cruise ship port-of-call, they were known for their superb diving, and with good reasons. The waters around them are, to use a vernacularism, gin clear. Visibility regularly runs from 100 to 150 feet, and occasionally exceeds an amazing 200 feet. If you stop and think about it, that's much clearer than the average swimming pool! Being near no other land mass, the waters around the Cayman Islands are simply as clear as the open waters of the Caribbean Sea. There is nothing like excellent visibility to fulfill a scuba diving tourist's dreams, but, understandably, there must be more, and the Cayman Islands have more — much more!

The Cayman Islands have both a unique underwater terrain and abundant marine life. Unlike most islands where the shoreline bottom gently slopes off into the sea over a great distance, these Islands are surrounded by great underwater cliffs called dropoffs. These sheer precipices generally start two to three hundred yards off shore, such as at Bloody Bay in Little Cayman. (Bloody Bay got its name from a fierce battle between the British and pirates when, as legend has it, the waters of the Bay ran red with pirates' blood.) The wall found there is renowned as one of the world's premier diving sites. Three Fathom Wall starts at a mere 18 feet, then plunges straight down for over 3,000 feet! To dive off one of these walls provides a unique sensation. You feel suspended in space with nothing below, and slowly you drift past colourful sponges, sea fans and other marine growth. Delightful tropical fish dart about like beautiful butterflies. Your bubbles may attract schools of silver horse-eyed jacks that rapidly swim in and swirl around for a closer look. At deeper depths, around 80 feet, you start encountering majestic black coral trees. At depths near 100 feet, you may start feeling the euphoria of depth-induced narcosis, but alas, this wonderful experience ends too soon as you must ascend.

In addition to the clear water and drop-offs, what makes these Islands especially unique is their sponges. Resplendent red cup sponges abound on the north coast of Grand Cayman, making it the "Red Sponge Capital of the World". On Little Cayman, there are yellow tube sponges so brilliant that they retain their colour in over 100 feet of water, although, at that depth, most colours normally fade. They are like none you will ever encounter any place else in the world. All three islands have huge barrel sponges that may reach an amazing seven feet in height. These huge sponges are well over 100 years old, as they grow less than one inch a year. Other types of colourful sponges, too numerous to mention, also abound in Cayman waters.

Between the shore and the drop-offs are interesting fringing and patch reefs populated by clouds of small, colourful reef fish. Angel and butterfly fish flit about the reefs foraging for food. Schools of grunts, creole wrasse, tarpon, horse-eyed jacks and others can be seen. Sea fans, sea whips, feather plumes and other gorgonians are especially abundant. Many of these reefs are shallow enough for snorkellers to enjoy, good examples being Eden Rock and Devil's Grotto. Just south of the George Town Harbour, these reefs are favourite places for cruise ship passengers to view the underwater world. Often, these reefs are cut by cracks, crevices and fissures where schools of silvery bait fish hide during the day. For the non-diver, a snorkel or even a glass-bottom boat trip can be a wonderful introduction to the underwater world of the Cayman Islands.

There is something mystical about shipwrecks, and divers are always attracted to them. In the Cayman Islands, the wreck of the *Balboa* in George Town Harbour and the *Oro Verde* off Seven Mile Beach are especially suited for divers. Lying in relatively shallow water, these wrecks have attracted large fish populations that are now supported, to a large degree, by diver handouts of food. Fish around these wrecks are so accustomed to divers that they show no apparent fear, and will even nip at a diver who appears on the wreck without an appropriate handout.

Yes, when it comes to diving, the Cayman Islands really have it all. Equally important to the seascape are the above-water support services for divers. Virtually every place of accommodation in the Islands will make arrangements to facilitate divers. Over half a dozen hotels must be classed as specialized diving resorts, and there are also live-aboard yachts that accommodate up to 18 divers. In addition to these resorts, there are numerous independent diving services that provide everything: learning-to-dive classes, daily reef trips, night diving excursions and underwater photography facilities are only a few of the services they offer. No other island in the Caribbean can boast the number and variety of diving services available in the Cayman Islands. The Caymans are indeed one of the premier diving destinations.

Yellow Tube Sponges at Little Cayman (opposite).

Feeding fish on the wreck of the *Balboa*.

Sightseeing the depths of Cayman waters by deep submersibles is now available to anyone.

The wreck of the *Oro Verde*.

Red Cup Sponges

Diving over a Cayman drop-off.

The *Atlantis,* a 50 foot long submarine, takes 28 passengers on underwater cruises to view the shallow coral gardens found on the west coast of Grand Cayman.

Divers entering Bonnie's Arch

Diving activities abound in the Cayman Islands. Virtually anything visitors may want in the way of diving is available, from being picked up in front of their hotel for a day of diving from a boat (left), to living aboard a diving yacht (below), to snorkelling from a dive boat or from the shore (bottom). It's their choice.

A scuba diver waves to passengers in a modern glass bottom boat.

Friendly stingrays of North Sound looking for handouts of food.

One of several modern glass bottom boats in Grand Cayman.

Tarpon at Tarpon Alley

Giant Barrel Sponge

Delicate tunicates growing on twigs of black coral.

The best asset of the Cayman Islands is its wonderful people. Warm, friendly and helpful are their trademarks. You will find virtually no racial strife or prejudice on these Islands, for they are a true racial melting pot comprised primarily of English, Scots, Welsh and Jamaican heritage. Generally speaking, the people are industrious, although they do move at their own pace (often called "Caribbean time"). Some outsiders may find this trait irritating, but many find it refreshing as it forces you to slow down as well. All of the above virtues must, at least in part, be a result of their years of isolation. The small population and lack of outside contact made it necessary, as a matter of simple survival, for the people to be friendly, helpful and industrious, all without the prejudices that affect the rest of the world.

Caymanians speak English in their own special and uniquely inflected way. It is obviously the result of many influences. Naturally, there is "British English" and typical "West Indian English". More surprising is a lilting inflection in their speech pattern that is credited to two early Welsh teachers on the Brac. Although most outsiders understand them without much trouble, there are several colloquialisms that may cause a problem in comprehension. For example, the expression, "that's finished". In the early days, when the arrival of supply ships was spasmodic at best, running out of an item meant it might be out of supply for days, months, years, maybe even permanently. Resupply was a matter of sheer speculation and thus the item was truly "finished". Today the colloquialism persists as a way of saying, "we are out of that product at the moment."

The Islands' population remained small through the years of isolation, and immigration was slight. Consequently, the majority of Caymanians descended from the same few families and carry the same last names — Arch, Bodden, Coe, Ebanks, Foster, Jackson, McTaggart, Scott, Tibbetts and Watler being good examples. Since last names were not a distinguishing factor in identifying a person, natives fell into the habit of formally addressing others by first name — Mr. Frank, Mr. Jim, Captain Charles, etc. The frequency of common first names also apparently became a problem and thus, new, one-of-a-kind first names were invented — Redfern, Tidyman, Fortesque, Convers, Minwell, Kemuel, etc.

The Caymanian people are, in general, deeply religious. Formal religion was established in the Islands when Presbyterian missionary, Reverend William Elmslie and his family, arrived from Jamaica in 1846. His mission was so successful that Presbyterianism remains the major religion on the Islands. One of the few remaining older structures in the George Town Harbour area is a church named for him. On the Brac, religion came with a Baptist missionary, Rev. W.H. Rutty, who settled there in 1886 and a shipwrecked Welshman, Jacob Josia Griffiths, who started a Baptist school. Other religions have since flourished on the Islands and numerous small churches and congregations can be found in all communities. On Sundays, the Islands literally close down with the exception of facilities operated for tourists.

Although there were some church-sponsored missionary schools, most notably the Presbyterian school in George Town, and the Welsh Baptist school on the Brac, education was, for many years, a matter of "catch as catch can". Individuals with even a little formal education would be hired by families to teach their children. Then, around 1910, the government began hiring teachers and set up schools in the various districts. They would teach children what was termed an elementary education, but, in reality, this education reached the level of high school. The brighter students often received special tutoring so they could leave the Islands for further education abroad. In 1920, compulsory school legilsation was passed and students were required to pass exams reaching the 6th level. This level was the equivalent of 8th grade in the U.S. today. Then, in the 1940s, both the Church of God and Presbyterian schools began offering true high school educations. In 1964, what was the Presbyterian High School became a public high school operated by the government. Today, education through both public and private schools compares favourably with any country in the world. Beyond high school, a student has the choice of going abroad or attending further educational courses offered by government and private concerns.

Like people all over the world, Caymanian people love to relax and play. Outdoor activities naturally include fishing, time at the beach and, in keeping with their tradition of seamanship, sailing. Ladies of the Islands are especially active with the gardens and resplendent testimonials to these pursuits are seen around their homes. Organized team sports are also big on the Islands. Soccer and cricket have always been popular, and more recently, rugby (British football) has also become an Island sport. Tennis and squash are both established sports and respective club courts are available. Cycling is becoming a popular sport among the younger generation. Less strenuous forms of play include darts and dominoes.

In addition to traditional English holidays such as Christmas, Boxing Day, New Years, Ash Wednesday, Good Friday, Easter and the Queen's Birthday, Caymanians have several holiday events of their own. Ash Wednesday is celebrated with an agricultural fair and other activities. Discovery Day is observed with a family fair and recreation designed for family participation. Constitution Day is a tribute to the Islands' form of democratic government. Pirates Week, started in 1979 to promote tourism, has become a true Caymanian festival with activities lasting a full week. The week starts with a flotilla arrival of pirates who capture the Governor and then parade through the streets of George Town, acting as though they are taking over the country. This is followed by parties, dances, evening fireworks and other activities all week long, including Heritage Days in each district.

FACES
OF
CAYMAN

Young and old in harmony on Little Cayman. "Uncle" Joe followed the old Caymanian tradition of being both a shipwright and seaman. He built his first of 76 boats in 1910 at age 16. Now in his 90s, he enjoys the company of little "Breezy".

A landmark in George Town, the ELMSLIE MEMORIAL CHURCH was built in 1923 by noted Cayman shipwright and builder, Captain Rayal Bodden. It was named in memory of the missionary, Reverend William Elmslie, the first clergyman to bring religion to the Cayman Islands in 1846. The cenotaph in the foreground is a memorial to the Caymanians who gave their lives in both world wars.

A modern education is available in the Cayman Islands through high school grades. There are both government and privately operated schools. There are also post high school classes offered by both government and private institutions.

Chemistry class (right)

First graders prepare for a puppet show (below)

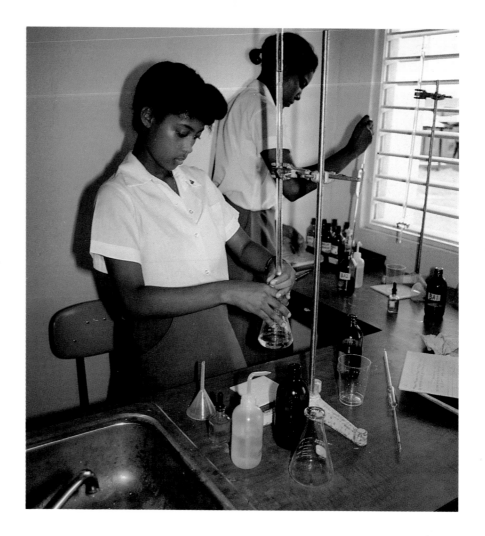

Computer class

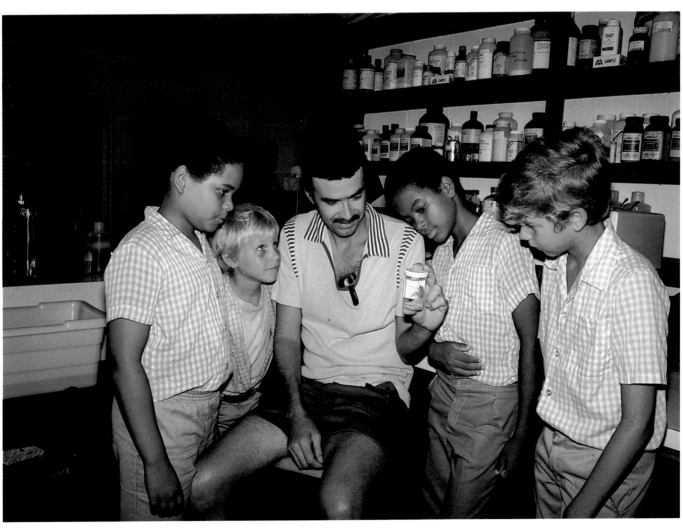

Field trip to biology lab at the Turtle Farm

Many a recreational hour is spent fishing in Cayman (right and far right). It is a sport that is learned at a very young age.

Team sports include soccer (below) and cricket (far bottom).

Sailboat racing is a regular weekend activity of the Grand Cayman Yacht Club.

Like any place in the world, family cookouts on Sunday afternoon are a tradition in Cayman. One of the most unique spots for such an outing is a shallow bar of pure white sand just inside the fringing reef in North Sound.

A spontaneous singing fest is an enjoyable diversion in "My Bar" at Sunset House.

Dominoes, a popular game, is played anytime, any place, throughout the Islands. It is played with fervour that demands the player slam a domino to the table when making an exciting play.

Despite the mutiny on the *Bounty,* breadfruit was eventually brought to the West Indies. It is still eaten today in a variety of delicious recipes handed down from generation to generation.

Combing the beaches for beautiful shells is a popular activity.

Caymanian children enjoy fresh coconut water.

The people of the Cayman Islands observe several local holidays in addition to traditional English Holidays. For example, Discovery Day is celebrated with a family fair and recreation designed for family participation (above). Pirates Week is a week-long festival that begins with the landing of pirates who take the Governor prisoner and parade through George Town (opposite page). The week is filled with special activities, parties and Heritage Days in each of the districts.

In 1671, about the time the first settlers were appearing in the Cayman Islands, the Treaty of Madrid was signed, giving Great Britain control of the Caymans. Jamaica, being the closest major British Island, was given governmental supervision of the island trio. With so few people inhabiting the Islands, nothing was really done about government until 1750 when a tyrannical ruler, William Cartwright, was installed. He was replaced in 1776 by "The Grand Old Man of Grand Cayman", William Bodden. Although not officially a Governor, he was called this by the people out of pure respect. Governor Bodden set up a democratic government and, under him, the Islands prospered. Like George Washington in the U.S.A., he remains "in the hearts of his countrymen". Direct administration from Jamaica, or help of any kind for that matter, continued to be slight. The Islands were basically left to develop on their own.

In 1962, Jamaica declared her independence from Britain. The people of the Cayman Islands, never having felt oppressed by the British and feeling almost totally ignored by Jamaica, voted overwhelmingly to remain a part of the British Empire. Thus, they became one of the few remaining Crown Colonies. More recently, a third-world-dominated U.N. commission on colonialism suggested that the Islands should become independent. The Island people not only rejected the idea, but indignantly told the U.N. to "keep their nose out" of Cayman's political affairs!

The people's continued loyalty to the throne was finally rewarded on February 16, 1983 by a 24-hour Royal visit to Grand Cayman from Queen Elizabeth II and Prince Philip. In addition to an island tour with numerous stops and receptions to visit with the local population, the Queen officially opened The Pines, the first old people's home in Grand Cayman.

Today, the government structure includes a Governor and Police Commissioner who are appointed by the Queen. But in reality, the Islands are ruled by the Executive Council and the Legislative Assembly. The Legislature is composed of 12 Elected Members chosen from six voting districts in the Islands, three Official Members and the Governor. The day-to-day administration of the country and the formulation of laws to be voted upon by the Legislative Assembly are the responsibility of the Executive Council. This Cabinet is comprised of three Official Members who are appointed by the Governor and four Elected Members from the Legislature. The Governor presides as Chairman. Normally, the Governor must accept the advice of the Executive Council except in matters of foreign affairs, defense, internal security and civil appointments. He may go against their wishes only with the approval of the British Secretary of State for Foreign and Commonwealth Affairs, in London.

The Cayman Islands' freedom from taxation is one of the most intriguing aspects of the Islands' economy. Just why the Islands were granted tax-free status (along with freedom from conscription) is an unsolved mystery. One of the most delightful legends explaining the status revolves around the Wreck of the Ten Sails at East End. On a dark night in 1788, one of a group of ten English ships floundered on the reef. Signals for the remaining ships to stay away were mistaken for an "all clear" and the whole fleet turned and sailed right onto the unforgiving reef. As the legend continues, the people of East End courageously rescued the crew and passengers which happened to include a member of the Royal family. In gratitude for their heroic deeds, the people of the Islands were granted freedom from taxation and conscription! It is a nice story and whatever the true source of the favoured status, its reality has had a profound effect on the Islands' development.

Naturally, the Government cannot function without money, so "tax free" has, in application, resulted in no income, sales or inheritance taxes. The Government gets its money instead from duty levied on nearly all imports. Nowadays, since virtually everything used or consumed on the Islands has been imported, the average duty of 20 percent amounts to a tidy sum. This duty is the primary reason that things purchased (other than duty-free) on the Islands are so expensive for, in actuality, it acts as a 20 percent wholesale tax. The Government additionally raises money by licence fees covering everything from businesses to drivers, and there are hefty work permit fees for expatriates. The Government also gets its share of the tourist dollar with hotel bill and airport departure taxes. Another large source of revenue comes from a 7½ percent stamp tax on all real estate transactions.

The single most important aspect of the tax-free status is the lack of individual or business income taxes. Since there are no income taxes, there is no need for the prying eyes of government to examine the books and records of individuals and businesses, or their bank accounts either, for that matter. Thus, in 1966, liberal banking laws were passed, ushering in, along with tourism, the present era of prosperity. To ensure the confidential relationship between bank and customer, the "Bank Secrecy" law was passed in 1976, making it a crime for a bank or its officers to reveal to anyone, anything about customers' dealings with the bank. Being a "tax haven", individuals, banks, trusts and off-shore corporations have flocked to the Islands to do their private business without the hassle of government scrutiny.

The Queen's Birthday is the largest governmental celebration on the Islands. The Governor traditionally leads the ceremonies.

There is always a large turnout for the Queen's Birthday Celebration.

Governmental awards of honour to outstanding citizens are presented by the Governor during the ceremonies.

The Queen's Birthday ceremonies start and end with a colourful parade.

After the Queen's Birthday ceremonies, everyone is invited to a reception at the Governor's Residence.

Laws Courts Building

Court in session

Appeals Court justices discuss a fine point of law with a Queen's Counsel.

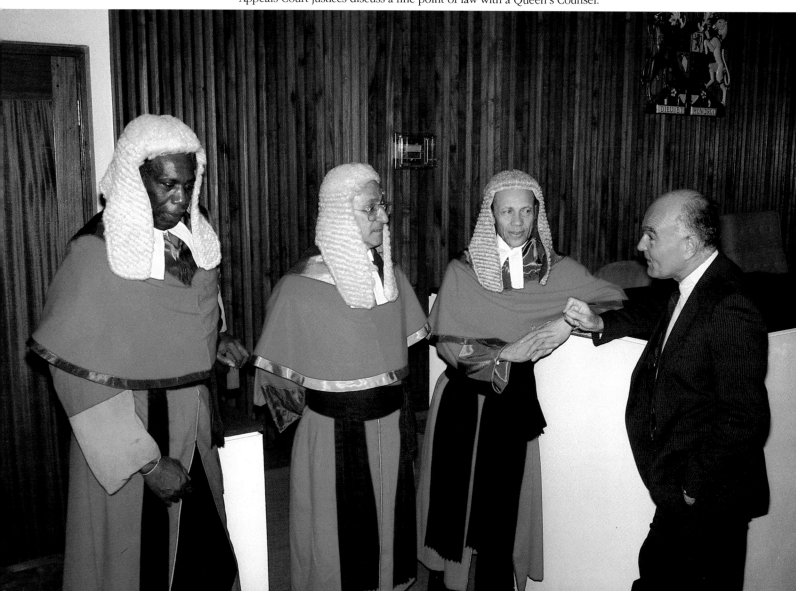

Government administrative headquarters, commonly called the "Glass House".

Governor's residence, located on the Seven Mile Beach.

Democratic government is presided over by the Legislative Assembly.

Legislative Assembly Building

HER MAJESTY QUEEN ELIZABETH II being greeted by the local population during a 1983 visit.

The abundance of giant sea turtles in the Cayman Islands were among the things that drew passing ships and eventually settlers to the Islands. Their meat was a rich food source for protein-starved sailors. Settlers commercialized the turtle, but because of the lack of any conservation efforts, the turtles had virtually disappeared from the Islands by the end of the 1700s. Fishing for turtles in remote Caribbean waters became the only way to continue this form of commerce. This required boats and thus, ushered in the ages of both boat-building and seamanship. Turtle fishing continued well into the 1960s. The end of the turtle fishing era was immortalized in Peter Matthiessen's best-selling book, *Far Tortuga.*

Boat building grew to become the primary industry on the Islands between the early 1800s and the early 1900s. Built of native mahogany and other woods, they were sturdy sailing vessels that were highly sought throughout the Caribbean. They were especially noted for their use of naturally curved woods, a sturdy alternative to the cutting or joining of timbers to shape. In fact, the ships were so well thought of that the last in a long line of shipwrights, Captain Rayal (Bodden), was commissioned by the U.S. Department of Defense to build three vessels for the World War II effort. World War II also brought an end to the boat building era. Native woods ran out, hand-built boats became uneconomical to produce and, although they could not be conscripted, many Caymanians went to sea as part of the war effort. The Caymanians' tradition of seamanship reached its peak during the three decades following the war.

During that period, nearly every man over 18 went to sea to earn a living. Their seamanship skills, especially in navigation and engineering, made them world famous and highly sought after. They sent their wages home, sustaining their families, the Islands' economy, and thus started the modern standard of living.

Women participated in commerce over the years by making baskets, rope and other woven goods from thatch palm. The rope, made from Cayman "iron" thatch, was found to be exceptionally strong and durable. In fact, Cayman thatch rope was reputed to be the best made in the entire Caribbean basin. Naturally, the rope was used by the boat building industry as well as being sold elsewhere, especially in Jamaica. For a good while, it was a major contributor to the Cayman economy. The rope and other woven goods would be made in the home and then bartered at the local store for needed staple goods. In recent years, with the availability of machine-made baskets, hats, nylon rope and other materials, the industry has virtually disappeared. Only a handful of women in the Islands still weave their thatch, which they sell from their homes and in gift shops as useful collectibles.

With the advent of regular air travel, reliable communication with the outside world, tax-free status and banking secrecy laws, came tourism, banking and numerous off-shore company and trust operations. Naturally, these forms of commerce need many support industries and businesses. Caymanians, being intensely capitalistic, have taken full advantage of the opportunities made available by these changes. They are coming home from the sea and abroad to take care of expanded family businesses and start new ones wherever they perceive a need. To assure Caymanians the chance of being involved in all aspects of the Islands' economy, law requires that they be the major part of all new businesses and operations on the Islands. Foreigners (called expatriates) are required to secure a "work permit" before becoming gainfully employed in the Caymans.

George Town, the Islands' capital, is no longer a sleepy little village. It bustles with modern office, bank and government buildings. It even has rush hour traffic jams! The road to West Bay is no longer a lightly travelled highway dotted with a couple of hotels and homes. It now carries a continuous stream of traffic past numerous hotels, condominiums and shopping centers. The building boom on Grand Cayman appears to have no end in sight and is threatening to spread to the Sister Islands.

Cayman Airways offers a regular inter-island schedule in addition to its international jet service to Jamaica, Miami and other major cities in the U.S. Additional charters are a necessity during the busy winter tourist season. The airline continues to expand, both in aircraft and destinations.

One of the most unique industries on the Islands is the Cayman Turtle Farm. Noting the decline in the world population of green sea turtles and the lucrative market for its products, a group of investors started the farm in 1968 with scientific help coming from researchers at the University of Florida who were partners in the project. Through research, they hoped to develop "in-house" breeding stock so the farm could become self-sustaining and perpetrating. As with many new businesses, time, money and projections all fell short and there was a series of changes in ownership. The staff remained, however, and continued their research, ultimately reaching their goal of being able to raise breeding stock in-house. Regrettably, with success so close at hand, the United States government delivered a nearly fatal blow by banning all turtle products (farmed or wild) in an effort to save the endangered world population. The farm, bankrupt again, was taken over by the Cayman Islands Government which has kept the operation and research going on at a greatly reduced scale. Ironically, although the U.S. ban for all practical purposes put the farm out of business, it may well turn out that the farm's research and stock population is the saviour of the world turtle population.

Recent agriculture efforts in Cayman include pineapple farming (opposite) by Franklin Smith.

Hybrid mangos are displayed by farmer Wille Ebanks.

With the advent of regular commerce with the outside world, farming almost disappeared from Cayman and virtually all food was imported. Today, agriculture is returning to help supply Cayman's needs.

Using irrigation, Franklin Smith is growing bananas and other tropical fruits.

Cayman Poultry Farm supplies fresh eggs.

Cattle farming has advanced to the point that John Bothwell specializes in breeding cattle by artificial insemination.

A visit to the CAYMAN TURTLE FARM is a favourite with tourists and a big event for school children as well.

Spontaneous fish markets appear on shore whenever local fishermen have had a good day.

E.A. Carter is the oldest store building on Cayman Brac. The indoor display cases and motif retain their 1930's period charm.

The weaving of native thatch in Cayman was once a full-time industry for women; today it is almost a lost art. Only a handful of women still weave goods to sell as useful collectibles from their homes or shops. Mrs. Jane Ebanks displays some of her handiwork at her home in Boatswain Bay.

Liberal Banking and Secrecy Laws brought to Cayman a full range of off-shore businesses, banks, trusts and corporations. To house this mushrooming industry, many new buildings have been erected (right and opposite below).

The TRANSNATIONAL complex includes luxurious office space, two restaurants, a hotel and convention facilities. The entire complex is centered around business.

Stamps from the Cayman Islands are a favourite among collectors throughout the world, making them big business as well as a source of government revenue.

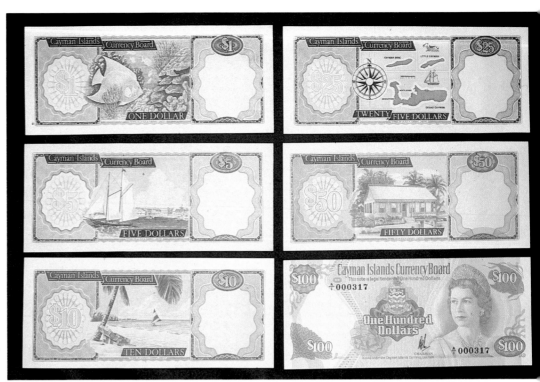

Each denomination of Caymanian currency is distinguished by a different colour; the bills' reverse sides depict local scenes.

Bustling port of George Town

Recently, a new ultra-modern terminal facility was opened at Owen Roberts Airport on Grand Cayman. Seen in the foreground is a unique display of aviation history in the Cayman Islands. An amphibian PBY, the same type used by Owen Roberts when he started air services to Grand Cayman, is contrasted with a modern Cayman Airways 727 jet.

Cayman Airways' inter-island aircraft at Edward Bodden air strip in Little Cayman.

Tourism got off to a shaky start in 1952 with the opening of the Islands' first hotel, the Bayview. The Galleon Beach Club (built on the current site of the Holiday Inn) became the first facility on the now famous Seven Mile Beach. Scuba diving was first introduced to the Islands by Bob Soto in 1957. In 1963, the Tortuga Club became the first hotel to offer diving as a regular part of its program. Tourism continued to grow slowly through the '60s. Then, in the mid-'70s, tourism took off and is still growing. In 1970, only 19,000 tourists visited the Islands; by 1987, the figure had increased to over 200,000 arrivals by air. It is estimated that one third of the visitors come specifically to scuba dive. In addition, over 250,000 cruise ship passengers visited the Islands in 1987.

The Cayman Islands have become a major tourist destination for several reasons. Probably the foremost is that it is a safe country, free from violent political turmoil and inhabited by friendly, English speaking people who want you to visit their Islands and make you feel welcome. Naturally, the availability of a wide range of recreational activities and attractive, comfortable accommodations are important factors. The consistently good weather throughout the year cannot be discounted. Finally, easy and relatively inexpensive access from the States by air is another consideration.

Naturally, water-oriented activities predominate the tourist scene. In addition to beachside fun and scuba diving, there are glass-bottom boat rides, party rafts, sailing, day-long boat trips to North Sound that include snorkelling and beach picnics, moonlight dinner cruises and so on. Recently, deep sea sport fishing has become a very popular sport on the Islands. There are several tournaments including "Million Dollar Month" during which a one million dollar prize is offered to an entrant who catches a world record Blue Marlin in Cayman waters. Little Cayman is not only known to have some of the world's best diving, but is also known for its world-class bone and tarpon fishing.

Other activities on the Islands naturally include sightseeing, and the time taken to drive around is well worth the effort. Although the distance is relatively short, a drive around Grand Cayman can take a full day, and maybe then some, if one stops at all the points of interest. Most hotels and condominiums have courts for tennis enthusiasts. In 1985, Jack Nicklaus opened Britannia, Cayman's first golf course. It is a short course designed as a new concept in island golf courses. To compensate for the short course, Nicklaus invented the "Cayman golf ball", a short-distance ball that makes the game as difficult as if it were being played on a full-sized course.

The most popular recreational diversion on the Islands is the truly beautiful Seven Mile Beach. Many visitors claim it is the best beach in the Caribbean, and there are several good reasons for that claim. Being on the lee side of the island, it enjoys consistent offshore breezes. This, coupled with the lack of offshore turtle grass beds, keeps the beach naturally clean and free of debris. The shining white sand is of a pleasing texture and slopes out gently underwater. The water is as crystal clear as you will find, and its colours are truly dazzling as they change with depth. On the beach or in the water, you can do most anything you want, from simply sunbathing and relaxing to swimming, water or jet skiing, parasailing and windsurfing. There are several beachside bars and outdoor eating facilities, so you can stay on the beach all day long and well into the evening with no reason to leave. Being on the west side of the island, watching the sun set from the beach is not only a tradition in Cayman, but also a wonderful way to end a day.

Relaxing on the white sands of the world famous SEVEN MILE BEACH.

On beautiful SEVEN MILE BEACH, one can enjoy most any activity, from a leisurely water buggy ride, exciting parasailing or jet skiing, sailing or windsurfing, to just playing, sunning and relaxing.

PLANTATION VILLAGE is one of the many beautiful condominiums built along the Seven Mile Beach.

There are several specialized dive resort/hotels in the Cayman Islands. An excellent example, SUNSET HOUSE is the only remaining local, family-owned and operated facility of its type.

The party raft KON TIKI offers music, dancing and party-making from George Town to the Seven Mile Beach.

Putting on the final green of the Britannia golf course. The clubhouse, in the background, offers a panoramic view of this unique course.

Little Cayman is world famous for its tarpon and bone fishing. A tranquil beginning to the day can be spent at the landlocked tarpon pond (top right). A fishing guide's "good luck" hat ensures results (top left). Hauling in a hard-fighting bone fish is always a moment of great exuberation (above).

The Cayman Islands are known for their excellent deep-sea sport fishing. There are several tournaments, the most famous of which is Million Dollar Month. Many a prize-winning Blue Marlin has been caught during this tournament.

The HOLIDAY INN facilities are a good example of the hotels along the famous SEVEN MILE BEACH.

BAREFOOT MAN, a local performer and songwriter for many years, spins out a wide variety of Caribbean-style music including many songs he has specially written about Cayman.

Relaxing at the pool bar is a favourite pastime at Treasure Island Resort.

Treasure Island Resort's nightclub is known for its outstanding entertainment.

A history of the Cayman Islands and the Caribbean during the days of pirates & buccaneers is presented at the Treasure Museum. Numerous artifacts, including treasures of silver and gold recovered from sunken ship wrecks, are attractively exhibited.

Bronze lions grace the reflecting pool and courtyard at the Hyatt Regency.

Ralph Terry makes beautiful objects out of native woods.

The making of BLACK CORAL JEWELRY in Cayman is a flourishing business that involves many local craftsmen.

One of the best ways to see scenic Cayman is by renting a car and taking a leisurely day drive around the island. Be sure to drive on the left!

Downtown George Town is a shopper's delight. Freeport shops abound, stocking exotic merchandise from around the world. Jewelry, gems, watches, perfumes, crystal, china and photographic equipment are only a few of the many things that can be purchased at bargain prices.

Hunting shells at sunset, a perfect way to end a perfect day.

Beloved Isle Cayman

O, land of soft, fresh breezes, and verdant trees so fair
With Thy Creator's glory reflected ev'rywhere.
O sea of palest em'rld, merging to darkest blue,
Whene'er my thoughts fly Godward, I always think of you.

Chorus
Dear verdant island, set in blue Caribbean Sea,
I'm coming, coming very soon, O beauteous isle to thee.
Although I wandered far, my heart enshrines thee yet.
Homeland, fair Cayman Isle, I cannot thee forget.

Away from noise of cities, their fret and carking care,
With moonbeams' soft caresses unchecked by garish glare.
Thy fruit with rarest juices, abundant rich and free,
When sweet church bells are chiming, my fond heart yearns for thee.

When tired of all excitement, and glam'rous worldly care,
How sweet thy shores to reach, and find a welcome there.
And when comes on the season, of peace, goodwill to man,
'Tis then I love thee best of all, Beloved Isle Cayman.

CAYMAN NATIONAL SONG
by Mrs. Leila Ross Shier